"THEY SAID IT!"

"THEY SAID IT!"

200 OF THE
FUNNIEST SPORTS QUIPS & QUOTES

ILLUSTRATIONS BY PATRICK MCDONNELL

Oxmoor House®

THEY SAID IT
SENIOR EDITOR: MORIN BISHOP
EDITORIAL ASSISTANTS: ROXANA LONERGAN,
    STACEY HARMIS
DESIGNER: BOB CATO

TO ORDER SPORTS ILLUSTRATED MAGAZINE,
WRITE TO: SPORTS ILLUSTRATED
SUBSCRIPTION SERVICE DEPARTMENT, P.O. BOX 60001
TAMPA, FLORIDA 33660-0001

Contents

ABOUT THE ARTIST

Patrick McDonnell's illustrations appear regularly in numerous national publications, including SPORTS ILLUSTRATED's weekly "Scorecard" feature. He is the author of *Bad Baby* (a collection of his cartoons from *Parents* magazine) and co-author of *Krazy Kat: The Comic Art of George Herriman.*

INTRODUCTION

All of us at SPORTS ILLUSTRATED were honored recently when SI won its second consecutive National Magazine Award for general excellence, an unprecedented achievement for magazines in our category—those with a circulation of one million or more. In announcing the award, the American Society of Magazine Editors praised SI for "its excellent photography, clean design and a collection of distinctive, writerly voices as varied as any in American magazines."

SPORTS ILLUSTRATED is indeed made up of many wonderful parts. Among the most popular sections of the magazine, and a personal favorite of mine, has always been one of the smallest and simplest: the weekly "They Said It" feature in "Scorecard," consisting of quips and quotes—often hilarious—from the leading sports figures of the day.

Over the years, scores of people have suggested that we publish a collection of our favorites. We agreed and here it is. As I read through the book, I'm reminded of the time Yogi Berra was asked whether New York Yankee first baseman Don Mattingly had exceeded Berra's expectations. "I'd say he's done more than that," he replied. That sort of sums up my feelings about this collection. Read on—I think you'll agree.

Donald K. Barr

PUBLISHER, SPORTS ILLUSTRATED

Say, What?

MALAPROPS & ODD VERBAL FORMULATIONS

———

■ *William Perry, the Clemson football team's 6'2", 305-pound freshman middle guard, talking about his childhood:*
"When I was little, I was big." *(1981)*

■ *Tug McGraw, Phillies relief pitcher, the proud owner of a 1954 Buick:*
"I like it because it plays old music." *(1982)*

■ *Caldwell Jones, Portland Trail Blazer center, when asked to name his favorite seafood:*
"Saltwater taffy." *(1987)*

■ *Harry Caray, World Series telecast announcer, describing the sound of the crowd as Bob Gibson neared his record 17 strikeouts:*
"The groan is audible. It can also be heard." *(1968)*

■ *Jim Wohlford, Milwaukee Brewer outfielder, on baseball:*
"Ninety percent of this game is half mental." *(1977)*

■ *Betty Richardson, after her third-place finish in the Delaware amateur golf tournament:*
"This game is 80% mental, and if you can conquer it mentally, you've got half of it beat." *(1976)*

■ *Dr. Bill Lenkaitis, New England Patriot center, on his budding dentistry practice:*
"It's all word of mouth." *(1977)*

■ *Rev. Dr. Felix B. Gear, of Decatur, Ga., newly elected moderator of the Southern Presbyterian Church, on his recreational activities:*

"I have hunted deer on occasion, but they were not aware of it." *(1964)*

■ *Yogi Berra, Yankee manager, on the American League situation:*

"The other teams could make trouble for us if they win." *(1964)*

■ *Chris Dundee, fight promoter:*

"I'd love to be a procrastinator, but I never seem to get around to it." *(1973)*

■ *Garry Maddox, Phillies centerfielder, when asked to describe his first grand slam homer:*

"As I remember, the bases were loaded." *(1976)*

■ *Casey Stengel, after sizing up the Mets' best pitcher in spring training camp:*

"Best thing wrong with Jack Fisher is nothing." *(1966)*

■ *John Lowenstein, Baltimore Orioles outfielder, suggesting a possible improvement in the game:*

"They should move first base back a step to eliminate all the close plays." *(1984)*

■ *Dan Osinski, Milwaukee pitcher, when a waitress asked if he wanted his pizza cut into six or eight pieces:*

"Better make it six. I can't eat eight." *(1964)*

■ *Yogi Berra, famous sayer of sayings:*
"I really didn't say everything I said." *(1985)*

■ *Bob Horner, Braves third baseman, on why he no longer sports a beard:*
"I've been travelling so much, I haven't had time to grow it." *(1983)*

■ *Benny Perry, heavily recruited strong safety from Bryan Adams High School in Dallas, on overtures from the scandal-plagued Southwest Conference:*
"You couldn't pay me to go to an SWC school." *(1987)*

■ *Mickey Rivers, Texas Rangers designated hitter:*
"We'll do all right if we can capitalize on our mistakes." *(1984)*

■ *Howard Cosell, discussing San Francisco Quarterback Tom Owens:*
"I'm impressed by the continuity of his physical presence." *(1974)*

■ *C.M. Newton, Vanderbilt basketball coach, misspeaking on a radio show about the loss of two Commodore starters:*
"We'll have to use some of our inexpensive players." *(1987)*

■ *Danny Ozark, Philadelphia Phillies manager, on his rightfielder:*
"Mike Anderson's limitations are limitless." *(1975)*

■ *Nestor Chylak, American League umpire, on why he did not eject Detroit Tiger Manager Billy Martin for his violent argument over the Bert Campaneris bat-throwing incident in the pennant playoffs:*

"I didn't see him do anything. After all, I've only got two pairs of eyes." *(1972)*

■ *Magic Johnson, marveling over how well he and Laker teammate James Worthy work together on the court:*
"It's almost like we have ESPN." *(1986)*

■ *Yogi Berra, Yankee manager, on the acquisition of fleet Rickey Henderson:*
"He can run anytime he wants. I'm giving him the red light." *(1985)*

■ *Leon Wood, New Jersey Nets guard, introducing himself to the team's TV commentator, Steve Albert:*
"Are you any relation to your brother Marv?" *(1986)*

■ *Johnny Unitas, during a discussion of longevity in pro football, reminded that George Blanda is even older than he:*
"That's because he was born before I was." *(1971)*

■ *Ralph Kiner, New York Mets broadcaster, during a recent telecast:*
"All of the Mets' road wins against Los Angeles this year have been at Dodger Stadium." *(1989)*

■ *Otto Graham, in an interview just before the Cleveland Browns and the Cincinnati Bengals met for the second time ever:*
"It will be a typical Browns-Bengals game." *(1970)*

■ *Jack Ramsay, Buffalo Braves coach, when it was suggested his woeful NBA team might be on the same timetable as the Cleveland Cavaliers, who had a 15-67 record two years ago:*

"We'll jump off that bridge when we come to it." *(1972)*

■ *Lou Spadia, 49er general manager, on the simplicity of signing Ken Willard of North Carolina, the 49ers' first draft choice:*

"We did it with a gentleman's handshake on the phone." *(1964)*

■ *Darryl Dawkins, Philadelphia 76er center, just before he took a vow of silence with sportswriters:*

"Nothing means nothing, but it isn't really nothing because nothing is something that isn't." *(1977)*

■ *Yogi Berra, Mets manager, after receiving a check made out to "Bearer" for his appearance on Jack Buck's pregame show in St. Louis:*

"How long have you known me, Jack? And you still don't know how to spell my name." *(1972)*

■ *Curt Gowdy, describing Dodger First Baseman Wes Parker on TV:*

"He was originally born in Chicago." *(1966)*

■ *Jack Kraft, Villanova basketball coach, commenting on a star player fouling out with less than two minutes to go and Villanova losing:*

"That was the nail that broke the coffin's back." *(1970)*

■ *Bob Veale, Pittsburgh Pirates pitcher, on the relative importance of pitching and hitting:*

"Good pitching always stops good hitting and vice versa." *(1966)*

■ *Shirley (Cha Cha) Muldowney, the only woman licensed by the National Hot Rod Association, explaining what motivates her to drive a top fuel dragster:*

"I want to be the fastest woman in the world—in a manner of speaking." *(1975)*

■ *George Rogers, New Orleans Saints running back, asked if he had any goals this season:*

"I want to gain 1,500 or 2,000 yards, whichever comes first." *(1983)*

■ *Stan Morrison, Southern Cal basketball coach, extolling the playmaking talents of Missouri Guard John Sundvold:*
"He's one of the smartest guys to put on sneakers since Einstein." *(1982)*

Coach's Corner

UNUSUAL THOUGHTS FROM THE SKIPPERS WHO MAKE THE CALLS

■ *Bill Parcells, New York Giants coach, on his run-and-shoot offense:*
"If my quarterback runs, I'll shoot him." *(1986)*

■ *Ed Temple, who has coached eight women's Olympic track gold medalists during his 38 years at Tennessee State:*
"I'm the only man alive whose wife approves of him going around with fast women." *(1989)*

■ *Stan Watts, Brigham Young basketball coach, asked if he intends to keep a pair of inexperienced 7-footers on his team:*
"Oh, yes. We'll really be impressive in the airports." *(1972)*

■ *Billy Tubbs, Oklahoma's basketball coach:*
"This year we plan to run and shoot. Next season we hope to run and score." *(1979)*

■ *Al McGuire, on his replacement at Marquette, Hank Raymonds:*
"My successor is a perfectionist. If he married Raquel Welch, he'd expect her to cook." *(1977)*

■ *Bob Zuffelato, Boston College basketball coach, explaining the pressures of recruiting:*
"Sometimes it's frightening when you see a 19-year-old kid running down the floor with your paycheck in his mouth." *(1975)*

■ *Bum Phillips, Houston Oiler coach, after passing a physical exam:*
"If I drop dead tomorrow, at least I'll know I died in good health." *(1976)*

■ *Frank Howard, Clemson coach, on college football players:*
"They're like tomatoes. When you get them they're
green, and you want to bring them along until
they're just ripe—you know, firm and ripe. They
can't get mushy. Sometimes seniors go to seed." *(1962)*

■ *Frank Layden, Utah Jazz coach, complaining about a former player of his:*

"I told him, 'Son, I can't understand it with you. Is it ignorance of apathy?' He said, 'Coach, I don't know and I don't care.'" *(1984)*

■ *Rich Donnelly, a Pittsburgh Pirate coach, on the preponderance of diminutive players on his team:*

"We have a shoe contract with Buster Brown." *(1987)*

■ *Marv Harshman, University of Washington basketball coach, explaining why he favors size over speed:*

"Quick guys get tired. Big guys don't shrink." *(1984)*

■ *Walt Michaels, New York Jet coach:*

"Everyone has some fear. A man who has no fear belongs in a mental institution. Or on special teams." *(1979)*

■ *Johnny Kerr, head coach of the new Phoenix team in the NBA, explaining why he declined the Chicago Bulls' offer to move into the front office:*

"I've seen enough guys who were kicked upstairs and then found out they were working in a one-story building." *(1968)*

■ *Former Denver Bronco Coach John Ralston, giving an explanation for his 1976 ouster:*

"I left because of illness and fatigue. The fans were sick and tired of me." *(1978)*

■ *Cincinnati Manager Fred Hutchinson, on armchair managers:*

"They've never been on a baseball field. Anybody can play ball in a saloon." *(1961)*

Pearls Before Swine

Bon Mots
from the
Clubhouse Philosphers

■ *Jake La Motta, former middleweight champion, on why the first of his six wives left him:*
"I clashed with the drapes." *(1985)*

■ *Steve Largent, Seattle Seahawks All-Pro wide receiver, when asked which record he will treasure most when he retires:*
"Probably the Beatles' white album." *(1987)*

■ *Elvin Hayes of the Washington Bullets:*
"I'd pay to watch me play." *(1978)*

■ *Bobby Bragan, Texas Ranger administrative assistant, after a home game against the Blue Jays that included a promotional appearance by Clayton Moore, the original TV Lone Ranger:*
"It's not very often we get to see the Lone Ranger and Toronto the same night." *(1981)*

■ *Chris Dundee, boxing promoter:*
"Middle age is when you start for home about the same time you used to start for somewhere else." *(1976)*

■ *Bobby Bragan, Milwaukee manager, on the reliance of baseball people on percentages:*
"Say you were standing with one foot in the oven and one foot in an ice bucket. According to the percentage people, you should be perfectly comfortable." *(1963)*

■ *Bum Phillips, Houston Oilers coach on being unprepared for sub-zero cold in Cleveland:*
"You can't practice being miserable." *(1977)*

■ *Harry Toscano, golf pro, asked by an acquaintance how he was playing:*

"I'm hitting the woods just great, but I'm having a terrible time getting out of them." *(1972)*

■ *Dan Quisenberry, Kansas City Royal reliever, on what happens when his sinker isn't working:*

"The batter still hits a grounder. But in this case the first bounce is 360 feet away." *(1980)*

■ *Rodney Dangerfield, comedian:*

"I went to a fight the other night and a hockey game broke out." *(1978)*

■ *Casey Stengel, after the annual Oldtimers Day at Shea Stadium:*

"Oldtimers weekends and airplane landings are alike: "If you can walk away from them, they're successful." *(1975)*

■ *Lee Trevino, who was once struck by lightning while playing a round, on how other golfers can avoid a similar fate:*

"Hold up a one-iron and walk. Even God can't hit a one-iron." *(1982)*

■ *Bill Lee, Red Sox lefthander, asked why southpaws are always depicted as flakes:*

"What do you expect from a northpaw world?" *(1978)*

■ *Pete Maravich, asked why he was taking the news of New Orleans Jazz Coach Butch van Breda Kolff's firing so calmly:*

"The last time I was surprised was when I found out that ice cream cones were hollow." *(1977)*

■ *Johnny Kerr, former 6'9" pivotman and now the coach of the Chicago Bulls, when asked by a woman if he was a basketball player:*

"No, ma'am, I'm a jockey for a dinosaur." *(1968)*

Good Point!

THE SOMETIMES AMUSING, SOMETIMES SERIOUS OBSERVATIONS THAT CONTAIN A GENUINE KERNEL OF TRUTH

■ *Sam Aubrey, Oklahoma State basketball coach, asked how he slept after his team's 83-62 loss to Colorado:*
"Just like a baby. I would sleep an hour, than wake up and cry for an hour." *(1972)*

■ *Brian Vriesman, 6'5" Hope College forward, on who had the most influence on his basketball career:*
"My six-foot mother." *(1975)*

■ *Bruce Crampton, on tournament golf:*
"It's a compromise of what your ego wants you to do, what experience tells you to do and what your nerves let you do." *(1976)*

■ *Gaylord Perry, Royals pitcher, 314 game career winner and reputed spitballer, on announcing his retirement at age 45:*
"The league will be a little drier now, folks." *(1983)*

■ *Rick Sund, Dallas Mavericks director of player personnel, after watching a halftime show in which a man juggled chain saws:*
"You have a turnover there, and you've got trouble." *(1987)*

■ *Gil Perreault, Buffalo Sabres center, naming the three most important aspects of pro hockey:*
"Forecheck, backcheck, paycheck." *(1982)*

■ *Eddie Arcaro, on what happens to the competitive urge after an athlete moves into the big money:*
"Once a guy starts wearing silk pajamas, it's hard to get up early." *(1977)*

■ *Michigan State Coach Duffy Daugherty:*
  "Football is not a contact sport—it's a collision sport. Dancing is a contact sport." *(1963)*

■ *Rod Gilbert, Ranger right wing, asked whether hockey fights are faked:*
"If they were faked, you would see me in more of them." *(1967)*

■ *Willie Davis, Green Bay defensive end, on the $15,000 he earned in the Super Bowl:*
"It's kind of like putting sugar on top of ice cream." *(1967)*

■ *Ron Meyer, New England Patriots coach, arguing that emotion is overrated in football:*
"There was a lot of emotion at the Alamo, and nobody survived." *(1984)*

■ *Mrs. Jeannette Baldwin, wife of Driver Ralph Baldwin, speaking of Hambletonian winner Speedy Scot:*
"I would have kissed him—but he bites." *(1963)*

■ *Betsy Cronkite, when told that her husband, Walter, an avid sailor and former anchor, wished to die on a 60-foot yacht with a 16-year-old mistress by his side:*
"He's more likely to die on a 16-foot yacht with a 60-year-old mistress." *(1986)*

■ *Vince Lombardi, general manager of the Green Bay Packers:*
"A real executive goes around with a worried look on his assistants." *(1968)*

■ *Howard David, a New Jersey Nets radio announcer, after the Nets acquired guard Mike McGee from the Sacramento Kings for second round draft choices in 1991 and '96:*

"I hope Sacramento is patient, because one of its picks is in the eighth grade now."

■ *Darrell Dickey, Kansas State quarterback and son of the team's coach, on Big Eight rival Oklahoma:*
"The Sooners don't rebuild, they reload." *(1980)*

■ *Chi Chi Rodriguez, on the sudden appearance of a transplanted tree on the 3rd fairway during the PGA championship:*
"I thought only God could make a tree, but I forgot about the PGA." *(1965)*

■ *General Dwight Eisenhower, asked if he noticed anything different about his golf game once he left the White House:*
"Yes. A lot more golfers beat me." *(1966)*

■ *The Kansas City Royals' 5'4" Freddie Patek, on how it feels to be the shortest player in the major leagues:*
"A heckuva lot better than being the shortest player in the minor leagues." *(1971)*

■ *Duffy Daugherty, Michigan State football coach, on hearing the suggestion that State's 42-16 loss to Washington could be attributed to the lack of traction his teams' shoes had on the artificial turf:*
"Blaming shoes for our loss is like blaming the Johnstown flood on a leaky faucet in Altoona." *(1970)*

■ *Bill Bradley, of the New York Knicks, on Atlanta Hawk John Drew's idea of making a movie of his own life:*
"Only one 20-year-old was ever worth making a movie about. That was Mozart." *(1976)*

■ *Gertrude Ederle, who swam 21 miles through New York Bay in preparation for her 1926 conquest of the English Channel, asked at the age of 66 if she could make the same swim today:*

"Sure, I'd float across on the garbage." *(1973)*

■ *Jack Lemmon, the actor:*
"If you think it's hard to meet new people, try picking up the wrong golf ball." *(1985)*

■ *Jim Tunney, NFL referee, offering his whistle's-eye view of the typical fan:*
"He'll scream from the 60th row of the bleachers that you missed a marginal call in the center of the interior line and then won't be able to find his car in the parking lot." *(1981)*

■ *James Maness, TCU wide receiver, after scoring a touchdown on an NCAA-record 99-yard pass reception:*
"This record is going to be hard to break." *(1984)*

■ *Ken Coleman, Boston Red Sox broadcaster gushing over a long home run by First Baseman Bob Watson:*
"They usually show movies on a flight like that." *(1978)*

■ *Mrs. Penny Tweedy, owner of Secretariat, on the chanciness of breeding:*
"Secretariat has a halfbrother who looks like a potential winner. But he also has a halfsister who couldn't outrun a fat man going downhill." *(1973)*

■ *Michael Jordan, Chicago Bulls Star, asked if he would be interested in playing golf with Detroit Pistons center Bill Laimbeer, whose handicap is one:*
"I'll play him as long as he doesn't foul me going to the hole." *(1988)*

■ *Heather Percy, mother of Karen Percy, Canada's bronze medalist in the women's downhill, confirming her daughter's reputation as a klutz:*

"I will never understand how she can ski down a mountain at 50 or 60 miles an hour, then come home and fall down the stairs." *(1988)*

■ *Beano Cook, University of Pittsburgh sports publicity director, on why an outstanding basketball player dropped out of school:*

"He got tired of his dad writing him for money." *(1961)*

■ *Beano Cook, a publicist for CBS Sports and an ardent football fan, after Bowie Kuhn gave the 52 former hostages lifetime major league baseball passes:*

"Haven't they suffered enough?" *(1981)*

■ *Jim Dickey, Kansas State football coach, asked to compare the 1971 and 1978 Oklahoma teams:*

"It's kind of like comparing the Atlantic and Pacific oceans. They'll both drown you." *(1978)*

■ *Joe Montana, San Francisco 49ers quarterback, asked if he'd want a son of his to play a dangerous sport like football:*

"Not if he can swing a golf club." *(1985)*

■ *Wally Butts, University of Georgia athletic director, speaking at the San Antonio Quarterback Club:*

"The definition of an atheist in Alabama is a person who doesn't believe in Bear Bryant." *(1961)*

■ *Bob Devaney, football coach, asked why he does not demand a lifetime contract from Nebraska:*

"I had a friend with a lifetime contract. After two bad years the university president called him into his office and pronounced him dead." *(1965)*

■ *Kathy Bosworth, mother of Seahawks linebacker Brian Bosworth, on her son's antics while growing up:*

"It's a good thing Brian was a third child, or he would have been the only one." *(1987)*

■ *Lou Henson, Illinois basketball coach, on why he is not recruiting Indiana coach Bob Knight's promising 6'6" son Pat:*

"I didn't want to pay him a home visit." *(1989)*

■ *Joe Paterno, Penn State football coach, asked if the highly rated Nittany Lions would be affected by the preseason press buildup:*

"I told them publicity is like poison—it won't hurt you if you don't swallow it." *(1969)*

■ *Jack Nicklaus, on why he tees a golf ball so high:*

"Through years of experience I have found that air offers less resistance than dirt." *(1974)*

■ *Candy Davis, wife of relief pitcher Mark Davis, marveling at her husband's new four-year, $13 million contract with the Kansas City Royals:*

"You'd think he discovered the cure for cancer or something." *(1989)*

■ *Willie Mays, paying tribute to Jackie Robinson, major league baseball's first black player:*

"Every time I look at my pocketbook I see Jackie Robinson." *(1977)*

■ *Karl Douglas, on his unshattered appearance after a poor performance at quarterback in the Colts' preseason game with the Redskins:*

"I try not to take life too seriously. You're not going to get out of it alive anyway." *(1972)*

■ *Ken Avery, Cincinnati Bengals linebacker, asked if anyone calls him a sissy because he studied ballet:*

"If they did, I'd stomp 'em and do a pirouette on their heads." *(1974)*

The Loser's Circle

THE VIEW FROM THE OTHER SIDE: MUSINGS FROM THE DEFEATED

■ *John McKay, Tampa Bay coach, asked following a 34-27 loss to Cleveland what he thought of his team's execution:*
"I think it's a good idea." *(1980)*

■ *Lou Rymkus, coach of the defunct Akron Vulcans, asked when he knew his team was in financial trouble:*
"When we couldn't get our uniforms out of the cleaners." *(1967)*

■ *Roger M. Blough, chairman of U.S. Steel, accepting the National Football Foundation Hall of Fame's gold medal, on his alma mater, Susquehanna University:*
"In the three years I played we won six, lost 17 and tied two. Some statistician with a great capacity for charity has calculated that we won 75% of the games we didn't lose." *(1963)*

■ *"Champagne" Tony Lema, winless in eight months:*
"It's been a long time between corks." *(1966)*

■ *Wayne Szoke, Columbia basketball coach, before the Lions' 68-49 loss to St. John's, the Catholic school ranked No.1 in the country:*
"It's a case of the Lions being thrown to the Christians." *(1985)*

■ *Chena Gilstrap, Arlington State football coach, on his team's low standing in the Southland Conference:*
"We've been in the cellar so long we've got watermarks." *(1965)*

■ *Terry Bradshaw, Pittsburgh Steeler quarterback, after nine turnovers helped Cincinnati upset the Steelers 34-10:*

"I just know the dog's going to bite me when I get home." *(1979)*

■ *Bob Betz, Longmont (Colo.) High School basketball coach, following a loss:*

"That was some of the worst fun I ever had." *(1983)*

■ *Mike Newlin, Houston Rocket guard, after a game his team lost to the New York Nets:*

"We were the quintessence of athletic atrocity." *(1976)*

■ *Benny Dees, Wyoming basketball coach, bemoaning a recent slump by the Cowboys:*

"It was so bad my travel agent called me with a play—and I wrote it down." *(1988)*

■ *Ken Brett, Chicago White Sox pitcher:*

"Things were so bad in Chicago last summer that by the fifth inning we were selling hot dogs to go." *(1977)*

■ *Former Yankee Pitcher Vernon (Lefty) Gomez describing his brief experience as a minor league manager:*

"We lost 14 straight. Then we had a game rained out and it felt so good we threw a victory dinner." *(1962)*

■ *Ben Crenshaw, golfer, on the pervasive quality of his current slump:*

"A couple of weeks ago I went fishing, and on the first cast I missed the lake." *(1977)*

■ *Matt McDonagh, 13, a soccer player for Highland Catholic School in St. Paul, Minn., after his team was eliminated by Presentation in the city's elementary school playoffs:*

"I knew we were in trouble when we got there and their cheerleaders were bigger than us." *(1985)*

■ *Bettina Bunge, tennis player, on what she has learned from her 11 straight losses to Martina Navratilova:*

"How to shake hands." *(1984)*

■ *Lynn Wheeler, after resigning as the coach of Iowa State's women's basketball team, which finished the season with 14 straight defeats:*

"I've taken this team as far as I can." *(1980)*

■ *Jack McMahon, Cincinnati Royal coach, asked what was the turning point when his team suffered a 109-95 defeat by the Boston Celtics and was ousted from the NBA playoffs:*

"When Bill Russell put on his shoes this morning." *(1964)*

■ *Bep Guidolin, Kansas City Scouts coach, asked if he has nightmares about his expansion team:*

"You gotta sleep before you have nightmares." *(1975)*

■ *Ken Plutnicki, Harvard forward, describing his frustration after the Crimson came close to beating heavily favored Duke only to lose 89-86:*

"It's like climbing the highest mountain and finding that the guru at the top doesn't know the meaning of life." *(1984)*

■ *Jack Harris, WFLA radio sportscaster, on Tampa Bay's offense:*

"They should put a sign on the 10-yard line saying, 'The Bucs stop here.'" *(1977)*

■ *Jim Fox, Los Angeles Kings right wing, complaining about the skating surface at a Culver City, Calif., practice rink:*
"I've seen better ice on my windshield." *(1988)*

Self-Portraits

PUNGENT SELF-CRITIQUES
FROM THE ATHLETES
WHO ARE
THEIR OWN WORST ENEMIES

■ *Mona Schallau of the Minnesota Buckskins, assessing her tennis game:*

"My volley is blah. I'm a dead elephant on the court. My serve has no sting and I am confused. Other than that I'm a fine player." *(1974)*

■ *Willie Mays, describing his new reaction to a knockdown pitch:*

"I stay down longer now to get rid of my mad." *(1965)*

■ *E.J. Holub, former Kansas City Chiefs linebacker, on his 12 knee operations:*

"My knees look like they lost a knife fight with a midget." *(1978)*

■ *Billy Casper, discussing the senior golf circuit on which he now plays:*

"Like a lot of fellows around here, I have a furniture problem. My chest has fallen into my drawers." *(1983)*

■ *Alex Hannum, Philadelphia 76er coach, asked why his height is now listed as 6 feet 7 when in his playing days it was 6 feet 8:*

"I got bald." *(1966)*

■ *Terry Hanratty, Notre Dame's star quarterback, after breaking a record held by legendary George Gipp:*

"I feel as if I just broke a piece of my mother's expensive china." *(1968)*

■ *George Keith, winner of the first annual Stone Skipping competition at Mackinac Island, Mich., where he skipped a stone 15 times on Lake Huron:*

"Ninety percent of my success is due to an astute selection of stones." *(1969)*

■ *Mike Eisenberg, 5'10", 220-pound basketball coach at New York City Technical College, describing the effect created when he stands next to his 6'6", 133-pound guard Martin Lacewell:*

"We look like the number 10." *(1989)*

■ *Fred Shero, Philadelphia Flyers coach, denying that he is unemotional:*

"I'm like a duck: calm above water, but paddling like hell underneath." *(1975)*

■ *Tom Watson, after being disqualified in the PGA tournament for changing putters in the middle of a rain-delayed round:*

"My IQ must be two points lower than a plant's." *(1986)*

■ *Hayden Fry, Iowa football coach, allowing that he's not much of a public speaker:*

"I'm the oratorical equivalent of a blocked punt." *(1985)*

■ *Miller Barber:*

"I don't say my golf game is bad, but if I grew tomatoes, they'd come up sliced." *(1975)*

■ *Arnold Schwarzenegger, six-time Mr. Universe, on what it is like to be beautiful:*

"Many times at the beach a good-looking lady will say to me, 'I want to touch you.' I always smile and say, 'I don't blame you.'" *(1977)*

■ *Bill Fitch, Boston Celtic coach:*

"I don't have an ulcer. I'm a carrier. I give them to other people." *(1980)*

■ *John Plumbley, Rice golf coach, on his team's erratic driving:*

"When the squirrels and birds see us on the tee they start scattering. We've set back the mating season in Texas 90 days." *(1970)*

Situation Comedies

Odd circumstances
that Made for
an Amusing Quip

■ *Mrs. John Sheblessy, referring to Cincinnati Bengal defensive tackle Mike Reid's recital before her music club :*

"He not only can play the piano. He can pick it up."
(1971)

■ *Jack Montgomery, assistant pro at the Ridgelea Country Club in Fort Worth, asked what he did when he spotted a couple of foxes on the golf course:*

"I reported them to the house committee — neither was a member." *(1964)*

■ *Butch Alder, Purdue football player, when asked how his conversion in spring practice from linebacker to center was going:*

"It's a snap." *(1981)*

■ *John (Beans) Reardon, former umpire, on receiving the Bill Klem Award at a Houston banquet:*

"I'm very glad to receive the Klem Award, but I'll tell you the truth. Klem hated my guts and I hated his." *(1970)*

■ *Ray Fosse, Cleveland Indians catcher, after he suffered a shoulder injury and was momentarily stunned when Pete Rose crashed into him in a successful effort to score the winning run in the 12th inning of baseball's All-Star Game:*

"Well, that's football." *(1970)*

■ *Len Jardine, football coach at Brown:*

"In my first game as a head coach I discovered there wasn't any chalk for my pregame discussion. I had to use my ulcer pills to write on the board." *(1970)*

■ *Tex Winter, Washington basketball coach, back from Fairbanks, Alaska, where the temperature fell to 50 below zero:*

"I don't think we'll be going back to Alaska. I've seen it. I believe it. I think I'll let it go at that." *(1971)*

■ *Charles Conrad, Apollo 12 astronaut, explaining why it will be fun to play golf on the moon someday:*
"Not only will you be able to hit the ball a mile, but because there's no atmosphere, you won't have a slice or a hook." *(1970)*

■ *Jake LaMotta, who recently married for the sixth time,*
commenting on his best man, Sugar Ray Robinson:
"He was the best man in our fights, too." *(1986)*

■ *Pete Carril, Princeton's basketball coach, after setting up*
two plays during a time-out and then watching as the
Tigers' Randy Melville threw in an off-balance 25-footer
with two seconds left to beat Cornell 46-44:
"It was the third of two options." *(1981)*

■ *Joel Hilgenberg, New Orleans Saints center, whose brother,*
Jay, plays the same position for the Chicago Bears:
"We're the only family I know that plays catch not
facing each other." *(1985)*

■ *Tom McVie, coach of the AHL Maine Mariners, on the*
cramped hotel room he occupied during a tam road trip:
"It was so small that when I stuck the key in the
lock I broke the window." *(1985)*

■ *Chuck Nevitt, the Detroit Pistons' 7'5" center, on growing up*
with a 6'7" dad, a 6-foot mom, two brothers over 6'7" and
a 6'3" sister:
"I never worried about whether I was adopted." *(1986)*

■ *Frank Layden, Utah Jazz basketball coach, reminiscing*
about his rough-and-tumble high school days in Brooklyn:
"We had a lot of nicknames—Scarface, Blackie,
Toothless—and those were just the cheerleaders." *(1986)*

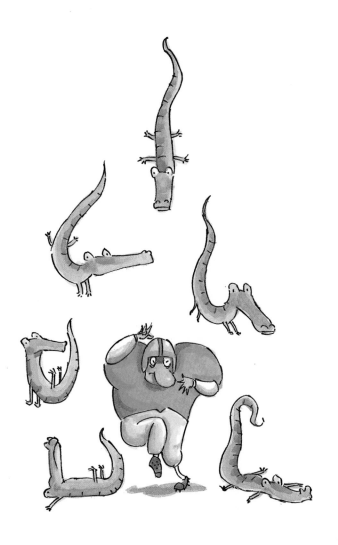

■ *Lou Holtz, coach of Orange Bowl-bound Arkansas, asked about fans who pelted the field with oranges during the SMU game:*

"I'm glad we're not going to the Gator Bowl." *(1977)*

■ *Jeff Feagles, Patriots punter, on his junior college team, the Scottsdale (Ariz.) Community College Artichokes:*
"We were known as the Chokes for short." *(1988)*

■ *Dean Martin, on the wagon during the Bing Crosby Golf Tournament, asked for his autograph on the 18th green at Cypress by a woman with green hair:*
"Lady, I knew something like you would show up the minute I quit drinking." *(1966)*

■ *Billy Herman, Red Sox manager, on who was the greatest brush-back pitcher of all time:*
"Freddie Fitzsimmons is my man. He once hit me in the on-deck circle." *(1966)*

■ *Ron Laird, U.S. race walker after he went off course in the Pan American Games' 20,000-meter walk:*
"I knew something was wrong when I came to a locked gate." *(1967)*

■ *Dave Graf, Cleveland Brown linebacker, on an ovation afforded teammate Dino Hall, who is 5'7":*
"When the crowd started chanting, 'Dino, Dino,' his parents must have felt five feet tall." *(1980)*

■ *Dick Stuart, Red Sox slugger, explaining to a traffic cop on January 2 why he still had 1963 license plates on his car:*
"Well, I had such a good year, I didn't want to forget it." *(1964)*

■ *Dick Farrell, conceding that the 32-degree Florida temperature might have helped his three-hit pitching for Houston:*

"It was so cold that ice was forming on my spitter."

(1964)

■ *Homer Rice, on being named head football coach at Rice:*
"When they said they'd name their stadium after me, I couldn't turn it down." *(1976)*

■ *Elvin Hayes, 6'9" Washington Bullets forward, asked in a hotel lobby if he was a basketball player:*
"No, I clean giraffe ears." *(1976)*

■ *Rocky Bridges, manager of the Phoenix Giants in the Pacific Coast League, after finishing second in a pregame cow-milking contest:*
"I didn't try too hard. I was afraid I'd get emotionally involved with the cow." *(1976)*

■ *George Webster, Houston Oiler linebacker, on his off-season job as a car salesman:*
"I haven't sold any yet, but I've been in field-goal range a couple of times." *(1969)*

■ *Doug Atkins, New Orleans Saints defensive end, on hearing that reformed teammate Joe Don Looney's dog had made a devastating raid on a hen house near Looney's farm:*
"I might have known. The minute the kid straightens out the dog goes bad." *(1969)*

■ *Bud Ogden, Philadelphia 76ers rookie, who made a perfect pass to the press table on a fast break in a game with San Diego, explaining to the writer who caught the pass why he threw it:*
"You were open." *(1969)*

■ *Jim Brown, of the Cleveland Browns, a 230-pounder, after being tackled by Obert Logan, 175-pound Dallas Cowboy safety back, and dragging him for several yards:*
"Man, you're just like chewing gum on my shoe." *(1965)*

■ *Jack Arute, ESPN commentator, when driver Jimmy Means lost a wheel near the end of a NASCAR race in Brooklyn, Mich.:*

"You picked a fine time to leave me, loose wheel." *(1986)*

■ *Mookie Wilson, Mets outfielder, explaining why he was wed in a ballpark:*

"My wife wanted a big diamond." *(1986)*

■ *Larry Kennan, Lamar University football coach, after Baylor attempted an onside kick with eight seconds left and a 42-7 lead:*

"Maybe they were afraid we'd run it back all the way, then line up and go for 30 points." *(1980)*

■ *Brook Steppe, Detroit Piston guard, after a game in the Silverdome:*

"It was the coldest gym I ever played in. A couple of rebounds came down with frost on them." *(1985)*

■ *Johnny Unitas, shrugging off news that Oakland Quarterback Dan Pastorini had demonstrated his throwing prowess by heaving a football from a hotel parking lot to a sixth-floor balcony:*

"His receivers were on the second floor." *(1980)*

■ *Jeff Lamp, Virginia basketball player, after 7'4" teammate Ralph Sampson dropped a throw that allowed the winning run to score in a campus softball game:*

"Ralph probably feels about 6'9" right now." *(1980)*

■ *Lew Burdette, Angels pitcher, asked about a batted ball which bounced off his leg and into the glove of teammate Joe Adcock:*

"This wasn't my best assist. I once started a double play with my forehead." *(1966)*

A Novel Opinion

THE INCONCLASTS SPEAK

■ *Barbara Romack, after playing a round of golf with Jack Nicklaus:*

"My tee shots felt like I was hitting overripe tomatoes." *(1962)*

■ *Dallas Cowboy Linebacker Thomas Henderson, on how exciting it is to be on a Super Bowl championship team:*
"I feel like a rat in a cheese factory with the cat on vacation." *(1978)*

■ *Bianca Jagger, discounting the importance of sex:*
"Unless there's some emotional tie, I'd rather play tennis." *(1982)*

■ *Lee Corso, Indiana football coach, who has eaten his share of chicken dinners on the post-season banquet circuit:*
"I no longer sleep. I roost." *(1979)*

■ *Carol Mann, golfer, on New Orleans Saints Coach Bum Phillips' crew cut:*
"It reminds me of a good three-wood lie." *(1981)*

■ *Steve Smith, world-record pole vaulter, noting that he has been vaulting half his life and yet fears heights:*
"If you put me up 18 feet on a ladder and asked me to jump into a foam rubber pit, I wouldn't do it." *(1973)*

■ *Glen Kozlowski, BYU co-captain and wide receiver, on the Mormon church's influence on the campus:*
"They let you chase girls, they just don't let you catch them." *(1985)*

■ *Dick Allen, on why he takes as little batting practice as possible with the Chicago White Sox:*
"Your body is just like a bar of soap. It gradually wears down from repeated use." *(1972)*

■ *Dave Lemonds, Chicago White Sox pitcher, on the Kansas City Royals' new Tartan Turf ball park:*
"It's like playing with marbles in a bathtub." *(1973)*

■ *Gary Player:*
"The ideal build for a golfer would be strong hands, big forearms, thin neck, big thighs and a flat chest. He'd look like Popeye." *(1974)*

■ *Joe Don Looney, Washington Redskin back, asked if he ever met a man he didn't like:*
"Yeah, Will Rogers." *(1966)*

■ *Joe Greene, who wears all four of his Super Bowl rings on his right hand:*
"Our motto is, 'One for the thumb in '81.'" *(1980)*

■ *Si Burick, Dayton* Daily News *columnist, on Secretariat:*
"He is everything that I am not. He is young; he is beautiful; he has lots of hair; he is fast; he is durable; he has a large bank account; and his entire sex life is before him." *(1973)*

■ *Ken Harrelson, former Red Sox outfielder and currently a TV commentator:*
"Baseball is the only sport I know that when you're on offense, the other team controls the ball." *(1976)*

■ *Dick Lynch, the New York Giants' radio color man, summing up the reaction of NFL rivals to Green Bay's acquisition of Wide Receiver John Jefferson to go with its other star receiver, James Lofton:*

"It's like finding out your mother-in-law has a twin sister." *(1981)*

Training Table

MUSING ON
ODD TRAINING TECHNIQUES
AND DIETARY HABITS

■ *Randy Miller, now a left wing for the AHL's Baltimore Clippers, on his previous boss, Springfield's Eddie Shore:*
"He was the most unusual man I've ever known. He had some good ideas and some bad ones. Like he used to have us tap dance on our skates during practice." *(1973)*

■ *Wilt Chamberlain on Philadelphia Coach Alex Hannum's training sessions:*

"If I can miss five minutes of one of his practices, I feel like I am adding five years to my life." *(1967)*

■ *Art Donovan, former 310-pound Baltimore Colt defensive lineman, describing himself as a light eater:*

"As soon as it's light, I start to eat." *(1980)*

■ *Kent Biggerstaff, Pirates trainer, on 240-pound pitcher Rick Reuschel's 4-pound weight gain:*

"Like putting just one more suitcase on the *Queen Mary*." *(1987)*

■ *Rocky Bridges, San Francisco Giants coach, on why he refuses to eat snails:*

"I prefer fast food." *(1985)*

■ *Nick Nicolau, University of Bridgeport football coach:*

"Our trainer has become so injury conscious that he is putting life jackets on the players before he allows them in the whirlpool." *(1967)*

■ *John Lowenstein, Baltimore Oriole bench warmer, on how he stays ready:*

"I flush the john between innings to keep my wrists strong." *(1979)*

■ *Bob Birdsong, winner of the medium-weight division in the Mr. America contest, on those who use oil to accent their muscles:*

"You gotta be careful. If you use too much, you look like a glazed doughnut." *(1973)*

Roasts and Toasts

WITTY CRITIQUES
BANDIED ABOUT IN
THE SPORTING WORLD

■ *Pat Williams, general manager of the Philadelphia 76ers, on 260-pound rookie power forward Charles Barkley:*
"Charles joined my family for a day at the beach last summer, and my children asked if they could go in the ocean. I had to tell them, 'Not right now, kids. Charles is using it.'" *(1985)*

■ *Orville Henry, sports editor of the Arkansas* Gazette, *on TCU Coach Jim Shofner, whose team has lost 18 straight:*
"He's such a nice guy. But if they had a Naive Bowl, he would coach both sides." *(1975)*

■ *Gary Player, on Lee Trevino's physique:*
"If he didn't have an Adam's apple he'd have no shape at all." *(1972)*

■ *Sandy Koufax, Dodger pitcher, on Casey Stengel:*
"When I was young and smart, I couldn't understand him. Now that I'm older and dumber, he makes sense to me." *(1966)*

■ *Bob Reinhart, Georgia State basketball coach, after hearing his team criticized by Oklahoma coach Billy Tubbs:*
"He's what's known as a contact coach—all con and no tact." *(1988)*

■ *Doug Russell, who beat the then unpopular Mark Spitz in the 100-meter butterfly at Mexico City in 1968, on Spitz' seven gold medals at Munich:*
"It could have happened to a nicer guy." *(1972)*

■ *Johnny Bench, Cincinnati Reds broadcaster, on the wide-legged stance of the Phillies' lanky Von Hayes:*
"He looks like a pair of pliers." *(1988)*

■ *Bryan Millard, Seattle offensive guard, on the toughness of Seahawk linebacker Fredd Young:*

"I would rather sandpaper a bobcat's butt in a phone booth than be tackled by Fredd." *(1987)*

■ *Charley McClendon, LSU football coach, on playing golf with Lee Trevino:*

"He's the only man I've ever known to talk on his backswing." *(1972)*

■ *Jim Camp, George Washington football coach, on why one of his stars didn't do well scholastically:*

"He is intelligent, but after eight minutes in class you could split his head open and about a thousand girls would run out." *(1966)*

■ *Gary Smith, Vancouver Canuck goalie, discussing 5'5" teammate Bobby Lalonde:*

"He'd be great in a short series." *(1975)*

■ *Jim Killingsworth, Texas Christian basketball coach, of Tulsa Guard Paul Pressey:*

"He's quick enough to play tennis by himself." *(1982)*

■ *Sandy Buda, Nebraska-Omaha football coach, on the Mavericks' 6'5", 257-pound defensive tackle, John Wayne Walker:*

"He's tougher than nine miles of detour." *(1982)*

■ *Lynn Shackelford, former UCLA forward, now a broadcaster for the Los Angeles Lakers, describing the size-22 shoes of Bob Lanier, Detroit Piston center:*

"He doesn't shine them; he sends them through a car wash." *(1972)*

■ *Gail Goodrich, the little giant of the Los Angeles Lakers'*
backcourt, when asked if he could see around Wilt
Chamberlain of the Philadelphia 76ers:

"Man, I couldn't see past his knee pads." *(1965)*

■ *Lenny Wilkens, SuperSonics coach, at a roast for General Manager Zollie Volchok, who is retiring in August:*
"I told him we needed an ultrasound machine and he asked me why we needed music in the locker room." *(1983)*

■ *Steve Garvey, on the gentlemanly conduct of Al Downing, his Dodger teammate:*
"If Al were dining alone, he'd still use his butter knife." *(1977)*

■ *Bill Muir, offensive line coach at SMU, on aggressiveness:*
"If the meek are going to inherit the earth, our offensive linemen are going to be land barons." *(1976)*

■ *Darold Knowles, Chicago Cub pitcher, asked if a former teammate was a hot-dog:*
"There isn't enough mustard in the world to cover Reggie Jackson." *(1977)*

■ *Pat Williams, Philadelphia 76er general manager, on 7'6", 190-pound Sudanese center Manute Bol, of the University of Bridgeport (Conn.):*
"He looks like he went to the blood bank and forgot to say 'when.'" *(1985)*

■ *Bruce Hurst, Red Sox pitcher, on his team's staff:*
"We have a lot of pitchers capable of stopping a winning streak." *(1986)*

■ *Rick Monday, Dodger outfielder, on Braves Pitcher Phil Niekro's baffling knuckleball:*
"It actually giggles at you as it goes by." *(1983)*

■ *Art Baker, the The Citadel's football coach, on Ronald Hale, Vanderbilt's 6'6", 310-pound offensive tackle:*

"I wasn't that worried about him until I read in their press guide that he was born on November 1st, 15th and 16th." *(1979)*

■ *Representative Joseph Moakley (D., Mass.), after lunching at the White House with Boston Marathon winner Bill Rodgers:*

"It's good to have a guy running in my district that I don't have to worry about." *(1979)*

■ *Marty Springstead, American League umpire, on former Baltimore Orioles manager Earl Weaver:*

"The way to test the durability of a Timex watch would be to strap it to his tongue." *(1984)*

■ *Milton Berle, at a roast of Howard Cosell:*

"Why are we honoring this man? Have we run out of human beings?" *(1984)*

■ *Field Scovell, chairman of the Cotton Bowl selection committee, on Bear Bryant's credibility:*

"If Bear tells me it's raining, I don't look out to see. I go get an umbrella." *(1974)*

■ *Mike Gottfried, Pitt football coach, on his referring to sports agents as "vultures":*

"I would like to apologize to the bird species for connecting these two." *(1988)*

■ *Mike Krzyzewski, Duke basketball coach, asked what he learned in his years of tutelage under Indiana's Bob Knight:*
"I learned to hate plaid." *(1986)*

■ *Lester Hayes, L.A. Raiders cornerback, after playing against the Eagles' scrambling quarterback Randall Cunningham:*
"He must shower in Vaseline." *(1986)*

■ *Bob Rosburg, pro golfer, discussing the Hazeltine National Golf Club course at Chaska, Minn. with its 10 dogleg holes:*
"Robert Trent Jones must have laid out the course in a kennel." *(1970)*

■ *Bob Costas, NBC sportscaster, on ageless New York Yankees pitcher Tommy John, 45:*
"This guy is so old that the first time he had athlete's foot, he used Absorbine Sr." *(1988)*

■ *Johnny Kerr, Chicago Bulls announcer, on 7'4", 290-pound Utah Jazz center Mark Eaton:*
"If you go to the movies with him, you get in for half price." *(1989)*

■ *Howard Johnson, New York Mets third baseman, on Royals slugger Bo Jackson:*
"Maybe they should see if his body is corked." *(1989)*

■ *Bill Pickens, 6'10", 270-pound defensive-line candidate with the Kansas City Chiefs after his first contact with their all-pro offensive tackle, Jim Tyrer:*

"It's like running into a brick wall that has arms." *(1967)*

INDEX